The Pyramids of Egypt

Kerri O'Donnell

Rosen Classroom Books and Materials
New York

Published in 2002 by The Rosen Publishing Group, Inc.
29 East 21st Street, New York, NY 10010

Book Design: Ron A. Churley

Photo Credits: Cover, p. 1 © Harvey Lloyd/FPG International; pp. 4–5 © VCG/FPG International; pp. 6, 7 © Kenneth Garrett/National Geographic Society; pp. 8–9 © J. G. Edmanson/International Stock; p. 10 © Chris Rainier/ Corbis; p. 11 © Staffan Widstrand/Corbis; p. 13 © Bettmann/Corbis; pp. 14–15 © Daily Tele./International Stock; p. 17 by Ron A. Churley; pp. 18–19 © The Telegraph Colour Library/International Stock; pp. 20, 21 © Gianni Dagli Orti/Corbis; p. 21 © Leonard de Selva/Corbis; p. 22 © Josef Beck/ FPG International.

ISBN: 0-8239-8236-X
6-pack ISBN: 0-8239-8639-X

Manufactured in the United States of America

Contents

The Pyramids of Egypt

Long ago, many **civilizations** built pyramids. A pyramid is a building with a square base and four triangle-shaped sides that meet in a point at the top. Some pyramids were used as temples where people could pray. Some pyramids were used as **tombs** where people's bodies were put after they died.

The pyramids of Egypt were built about 4,500 years ago. Today, the remains of these pyramids can still be seen near the Nile River.

The most famous pyramids are the pyramids of Egypt. Egypt is a country in northeastern Africa. The Egyptian pyramids were used as tombs for Egyptian kings. **Ancient** Egyptians believed in many gods and goddesses. They also believed that when a person died, his or her **spirit** continued to live. This spirit traveled to another world to live with the gods. The Egyptians believed that the bodies of their kings had to be protected so their souls could live forever.

Egypt →

Africa

The ancient Egyptians believed that their kings were gods who lived on Earth. A pyramid would be built while

These jars held the internal organs of ancient Egyptian kings.

This photo shows a burial jar found within the tomb of an Egyptian king.

the king was still alive so that it would be ready when the king died. A pyramid took many years to build. When the king died, he was buried inside or beneath the pyramid in a secret **chamber** filled with gold, **jewels**, furniture, and food that he would need in the next world. Thieves often broke into the tombs to steal these riches.

Many people think that the shape of the pyramids had a **religious** purpose. The sloped sides of the pyramid may have stood for the rays of the sun. The king's spirit could use the pyramid's sloped sides to climb to the heavens. Then he could take his place among the gods.

The sloped sides of the pyramid may have stood for the rays of the sun.

The First Pyramid

The oldest known pyramid was built for King Zoser (ZOH-sir) more than 4,600 years ago. The pyramid still stands where the ancient city of Memphis (MEM-fiss) once was. The city that is near there today is called Saqqara (suh-KAR-uh).

Historians believe that a man named Imhotep (im-HO-tep) made up the plan for this pyramid. Imhotep handled many of King Zoser's affairs.

The Egyptians came to think of Imhotep as a god of **wisdom**.

The pyramid he created for King Zoser was called a "step pyramid." The four sides of the pyramid are made up of six large steps built out of blocks of **limestone**. The ancient Egyptians may have believed that King Zoser's spirit could climb to heaven using the steps of his burial pyramid.

At 200 feet high, the step pyramid at Saqqara is the earliest known stone building of its size anywhere in the world.

King Zoser's burial chamber and storage rooms were carved out of the earth beneath the pyramid. The burial chamber was built to look like King Zoser's palace so that his spirit would feel comfortable. The rooms that surrounded the burial chamber probably contained King Zoser's furniture, gold, and other objects he might need when his spirit went to live with the gods.

The burial chambers of many pyramids were built to look like a royal palace so the king's spirit would feel at home.

Stone walls and doors between the pyramid's rooms were covered with ancient Egyptian writing. These were not real doors—the Egyptians believed that King Zoser's spirit would be able to move around the rooms of his pyramid without the help of actual doorways.

The walls and doors of many Egyptian burial chambers are covered with ancient Egyptian writing.

The Pyramids of Giza

The pyramids of Giza (GEE-zuh) are near Cairo (KY-roh), Egypt, on the western bank of the Nile River. The ten pyramids at Giza were built for Egyptian kings between 2600 B.C. and 2500 B.C.

The pyramids at Giza were made from large blocks of limestone. The ancient Egyptians used **chisels** and saws to cut the limestone into blocks. Large groups of men sometimes had to drag the heavy blocks from many miles away. After the first layer of blocks was pushed into place, the men probably built long ramps and dragged the blocks up the ramps to form the next layer.

These pyramids were different from King Zoser's step pyramid. Their sides were built to look as if they had been cut from one single, smooth stone.

It may have taken ten years just to build the ramp needed to build one of the pyramids at Giza.

The pyramids at Giza include three of the biggest and least damaged of all the Egyptian pyramids. The largest of the three is the pyramid built for King Khufu (KOO-foo). This pyramid is known as the Great Pyramid. The base of this pyramid covers about thirteen acres. The Great Pyramid was built with more than 2 million limestone blocks and was originally 481 feet high. Today, some of the top stones are missing, and the pyramid is about 450 feet high.

Historians believe that it took about thirty years to build the Great Pyramid. A large crew of workers probably worked on the pyramid all year long.

When the Nile River flooded the nearby fields in late summer and early fall, farmers and villagers couldn't work. They helped build the pyramid instead.

The pyramids at Giza are considered one of the Seven Wonders of the Ancient World.

King Khufu's burial chamber and many other rooms are inside the Great Pyramid. One room is called the Queen's Chamber, but this is not where the queen was buried. The room was originally supposed to be King Khufu's burial chamber, but he decided to build a different burial chamber. He may have done this to make sure thieves could not find and steal his burial objects. The plan didn't work. Thieves broke into his tomb and stole his body and his burial riches.

A hallway called the Grand **Gallery** leads to the burial chamber, which is known as the King's Chamber. The Grand Gallery is 153 feet long and 28 feet high. It is considered a great work of ancient building.

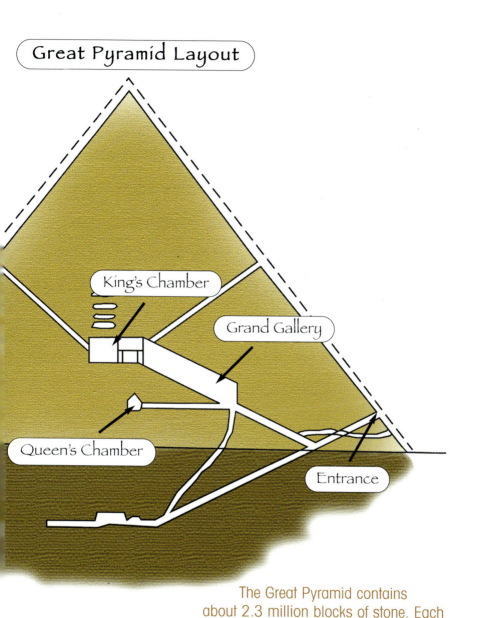

Great Pyramid Layout

King's Chamber

Grand Gallery

Queen's Chamber

Entrance

The Great Pyramid contains about 2.3 million blocks of stone. Each stone weighs about 2.5 tons!

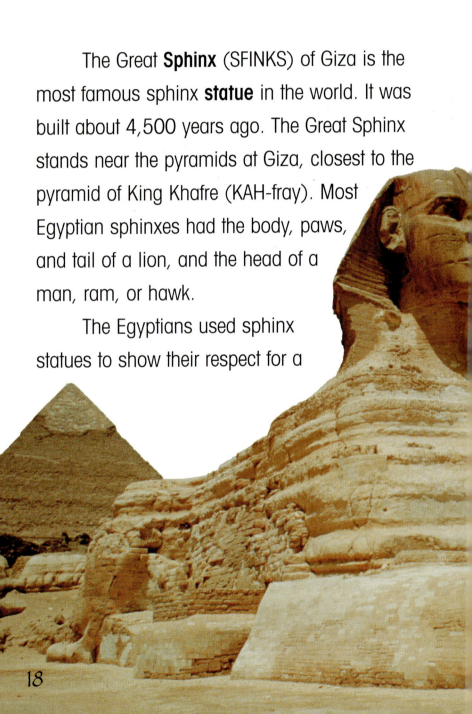

The Great **Sphinx** (SFINKS) of Giza is the most famous sphinx **statue** in the world. It was built about 4,500 years ago. The Great Sphinx stands near the pyramids at Giza, closest to the pyramid of King Khafre (KAH-fray). Most Egyptian sphinxes had the body, paws, and tail of a lion, and the head of a man, ram, or hawk.

The Egyptians used sphinx statues to show their respect for a king or queen. In Egyptian art, kings were often shown as lions winning battles against enemies. A sphinx became a sign of royalty, strength, and wisdom. A sphinx's face was made to look like the person whom the statue honored. Many historians think the Great Sphinx's face was made to look like King Khafre, who may have had the statue built in his honor.

"Sphinx" is a Greek word for a kind of monster. When the ancient Greeks visited Egypt, they used the word "sphinx" to describe the large stone statues they saw there.

Changing Ways

Thieves wanted the gold, jewels, and other riches that were buried inside the pyramids with the kings' bodies. They broke into the pyramids

Underground chamber of a pyramid at Giza

and stole what they found inside. Sometimes they even stole or destroyed the kings' bodies. The Egyptians built secret **passages** and rooms in the pyramids to confuse thieves, but this did not work. The thieves still found the kings' burial chambers and stole the objects they found there.

Since the pyramids did not protect the kings' bodies and burial riches from thieves, the Egyptians finally

A passage inside the Great Pyramid

stopped using the pyramids as tombs for their kings. Instead, kings were buried in secret tombs cut into rock cliffs.

Interior of Egyptian pyramid

The Pyramids Today

The Egyptians were one of the first groups of people to develop a religious belief in life after death. They left behind grand **monuments** that

continue to tell the stories of the kings, queens, and people of a great civilization that existed 4,500 years ago.

Thousands of people visit the pyramids at Giza every year.

Egypt's dry, warm weather has helped to preserve these ancient monuments. Today, visitors from all over the world travel to Egypt to experience the beauty and wonder of the pyramids.

Glossary

ancient   Very old.

chamber   A room.

chisel   A metal tool with a sharp edge used to cut wood, stone, or metal.

civilization   A culture that has a system of writing and keeps written records.

gallery   A large hall, room, or building.

historian   Someone who studies things that happened in the past.

jewel   A valuable stone.

limestone   A rock made mostly of the remains of shells and coral.

monument   Something set up to honor a person or event.

passage   A hall or way through a building.

religious   Honoring a god or gods.

sphinx   A statue of a lion's body with the head of a man, ram, or hawk.

spirit   The soul.

statue   A work of art that is shaped like a person, animal, or other figure.

tomb   A large grave that is built above ground.

wisdom   Knowledge and good judgment.

Index